THE ALL NEW STYLE OF MAGAZINE-BOOKS

SDMLIVE®

www.SDMLIVE.com

MP

MOCY PUBLISHING
WWW.MOCYPUBLISHING.COM

SDM LIVE ®

EDITOR-IN-CHIEF
D. "Casino" Bailey
casino@sdmlive.com

EDITORIAL DIRECTOR
Sheree Cranford
sheree@sdmlive.com

GRAPHIC/WEB DESIGNER
D. "Casino" Bailey
casino@sdmlive.com

ACCOUNT EXECUTIVE
Frank Harvest Jr.
frank@sdmlive.com

PHOTOGRAPHERS
Anterlon Terrell Fritz
Treagen Colston
Terance Drake

CONTRIBUTORS
April Smiley
Courtney Benjamin

COPY ORDERS & ADVERTISING OFFICE
Send Money Order or Check to:
Mocy Publishing
P.O. Box 35195
Detroit, Michigan 48235
(586) 646-8505
advertise@sdmlive.com

Copy Order Item
SDM Live Magazine Issue #13
S&H Plus Retail Price - $9.99 per copy

WWW.SDMLIVE.COM

Printed by CreateSpace, An Amazon.com Company

MP
MOCY PUBLISHING

REAL MUSIC. REAL ENTERTAINMENT.
SDM
ISSUE #13

Also
RAIL FRESH
GUCCI RIE
BRIAA DUPREE
PAULETTE GREEN
CYNASURE RENAE

CHAMERE
THE GLAM PRINCESS

NEW
AKINYELE THE BLK NIGHT
TAKING R&B INDIE MUSIC TO NEW LEVELS

FRANK FISHER
FINDING THE KEYS TO BEING MORE THAN JUST AN ARTIST

WWW.SDMLIVE.COM

CONTENTS

1

Sony - 65" Class (64.5" Diag.) - 2160p Smart - 4K Ultra HD TV with High Dynamic Range - Black
$1399.99
www.bestbuy.com

2

Roku - Premiere Streaming Media Player - Black
$69.99
www.bestbuy.com

3

Epson - WorkForce DS-30 Portable Document Scanner - Black
$79.99
www.bestbuy.com

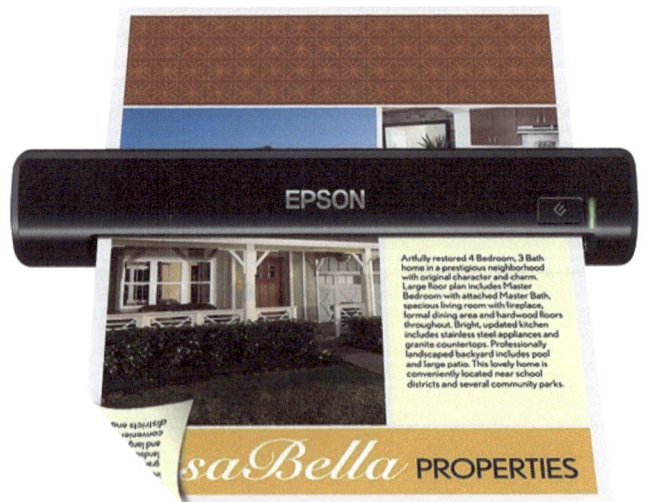

No Guns Allowed

FEMALE RAPPER MOLLY BRAZY IS WALKING ON THIN ICE AS INVESTIGATORS PREP TO STICK HER WITH A CRIME & SOME TIME FOR USING GUN VIOLENCE.

by Cheraee C.

Image is everything and rappers tend to forget how quickly one video can go viral. Even though Detroit femcee Molly Brazy didn't post this alleged video herself that has the media on 1000, she's the number one suspect in it. Molly is currently the talk of the town, the internet, blogs, newsfeeds and so forth. She's currently under investigation for aiming a gun at a toddler's head.

Molly Brazy is only 18 years old, but since she has a net worth and she's a signed artist she should have some respect for herself, the toddler, and her reputation. She's old enough to be charged and tried as an adult. Who cares whether the gun is real or fake? Where did Molly get the weapon from? Why was she playing with the weapon around a toddler? What if the weapon was armed and had killed or injured someone?

Molly's manager claims she was playing with the toddler and the toddler was playing with her. Where do toddlers play with guns, and people use guns to play with toddlers at? There is no way that CPS or DPD shouldn't be all over this case. If anything Molly should've been rapping, dancing, playing with Barbies, or having a tea party doing age appropriate activities with the toddler. Our younger generations idolize people like Molly who become successful at a young age. No youthful role model should have controversy about guns and toddlers. Whether you're a rapper or a millionaire that might buy you a bail, but it cannot uncharge the crime or the time. If Molly is guilty of criminal offenses from this video hopefully justice is served and she becomes a spokesperson for why you shouldn't play with guns. How would she had felt if a gun was pointed at her head?

Love Triangles Exist

AMINA PANKEY A MARRIED, REALTY STAR TELLS HER STORY IN A JUICY TELL ALL BOOK REVEALING HER COMPLICATED LOVE LIFE.
by Cheraee C.

Amina Pankey also known in the industry as Amina Buddafly thought she was marrying her soulmate only to find out she was entering into a deceptive, love triangle. Peter Gunz used his womanizing skills to play both sides of the fence with his baby mother Tara and his wife Amina.

Instead of peeping game and ending this malicious relationship with Mr. Gunz Amina continues to fuel a relationship with Mr. Gunz. This love triangle has been on national TV for at least four years. How much forgiving and backstabbing does it take to end a relationship?

Just because a woman enters into a marriage doesn't mean there is no exit wounds. In life, people are only going to do what you allow them to do. It doesn't matter if you are from Neptune, you should never settle for less of what you deserve or what you expect. Fasten your eyes and read all about Amina's love tale in her new book "The Other Woman."

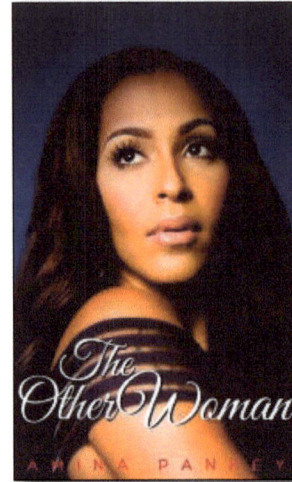

The Other Women
By Amina Pankey

Available from Amazon.com and other online stores

COMING SOON!!!

A BOOK OF SHORT STORIES & POETRY

Brown Paper Suga

forwarded by
Cheraee C.

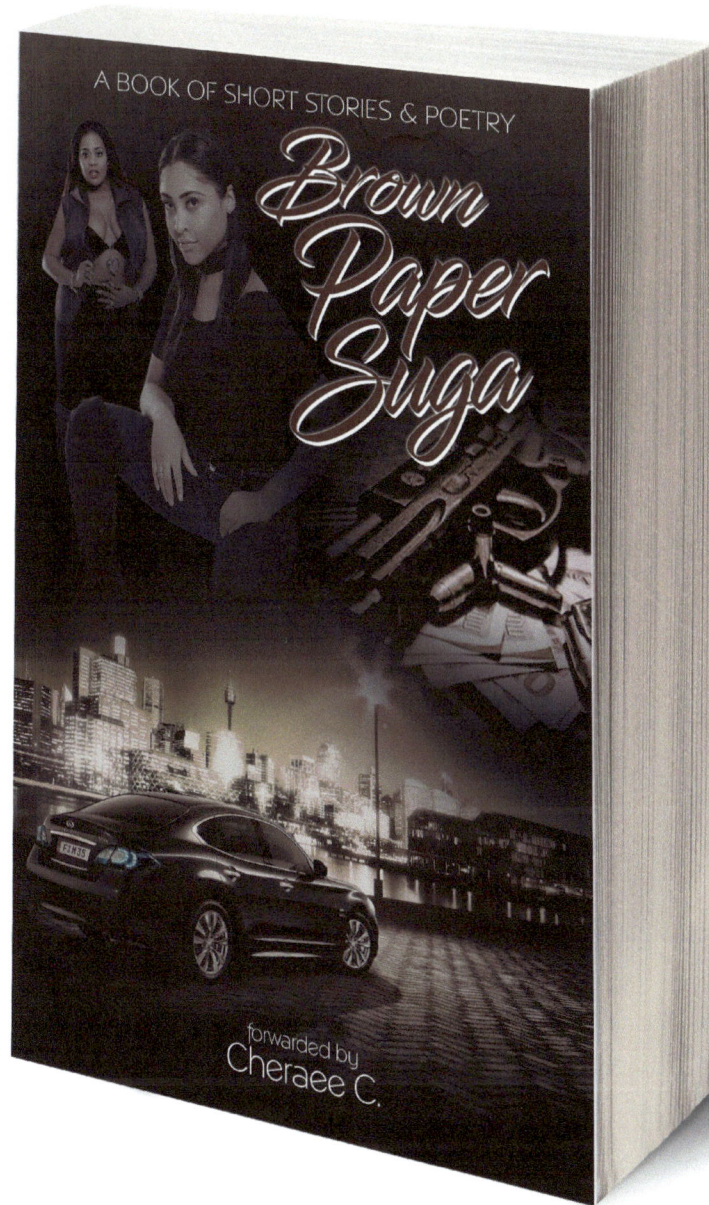

Brown Paper Suga
By Cheraee C.

More Than Just an Artist

ARTIST FRANK FISHER CONTINUES TO PUT UNDERGROUNG R&B ON THE MAP WITH HIS LATEST TWO SINGLES "YO FREAM" AND "ADDICTED"

by Cheraee C.

Q. What is your opinion of the R&B scene in Detroit? How do you feel about the underground scene? You think it's overcrowded?

A. I feel like there's a lot of artists that don't get enough recognition if any. The underground scene is very overcrowded and at times that makes it hard for artists like me.

Q. Since you been on the scene anything ever make you want to give up? What keeps you motivated? What's your goal for your music career this year and what areas are you focusing on?

A. Losing my mother was a big hit too me while dealing with other life issues, but I could never give up doing music because I just love it too much and I'm too great at what I do to stop. I don't wanna lose my God given gifts or my progress. Just being successful and working with as many artists as I can as a producer and an artist.

Q. What do you do in your spare time when your not producing or singing?

A. Getting a check to be honest. I'm always working on music and some days I barely sleep working with artists and working on my stuff. I don't really like to waste time and I don't like to just be looked a as a singer I just call myself an artist because my music is versatile, but I'm not a rapper either I'm just me. I book studio time daily for many artists in my city. I'm starting to become a business lol. People always need beats and a dope engineer.

Q. What would you say is the best song you've produced for an artist and yourself?

A. The best song I've produced for an artist this far was "Trap Stack Pray" for my bro B Dot (@Trualienbdot.) He out in Atlanta preparing to do some big things and so will you. I will have to say the best song I've produced for myself was my single "Band Dance." A lot of people love that song.

Q. How did you end up getting involved with DJ Hollyhood and his project Romie Must Die?

A. DJ Hollyhood hmu and asked me to send him sum tracks for the tape so I sent him a couple of my new joints "Yo Freak" and "Addicted." He's gonna be hosting a few projects for me to.

Strut Your Stuff

RIPPING RUNWAYS AND SLAYING FASHION SHOWS AROUND THE COUNTRY IS THE LIFESTYLE OF CURVY, TOP MODEL CYNASURE RENAE.

by Cheraee C.

Q. How did you learn how to model and what is your best part about modeling?

A. Foremost my grandmother Helen Corr taught me poise, posture, and grace as a child. As an adult, I gained skills and formal training from the best names in Runway Coaching and Etiquette who are Jeremy Cornelius of Jer DeCor and Runway Rox!

Q. What famous and/or underground models do you admire most and why?

A. Mia Amber Davis for her bigger then life sweetness on film and calm and grace on the runway. Tiffany Stewart as she was a lovely example firsthand in my first runway experiences of what I strived to be on the runway tight, smooth, and poised. A model @_kamora_ on her boldness and strength in photos that displays beautifully how you embraace and show the curves and edges society teaches you to hide.

Q. Currently what photographer do you enjoy working with the most and why?

A. So far I have most enjoyed working with Terance Drake. He was instrumental throughout a 6-7 month calender project titled #bigsexzifromthecalenderfirstedition, wherein he went above and beyond to give instruction, guidance, and training on editorial shoots and poses.

Q. Tell us the craziest experience you've had on a photo shoot?

A. My craziest experience I'll share is shooting at the Dequindre Cut last summer after climbing up in the arches after dark for poses and looking to see my arch enemy and fear, giant spiders strewn about above my head! Listen! The adrenaline rush to flee the scene was instant! Yet the immense level of composure needed to squelch that to avoid losing the shots and breaking my ankles in heels was a lesson in overcoming a fear through necessity.

Q. How did you meet the Glam Princess Chamere?

A. I met her through The Walk Fashion Show. The Walk Organization is where I started runway professionally and she was the glamorous designer that brought the glitter glory and wings to the runway honey! I became acquainted by proximity in the fashion shows and fellow models. As I developed my craft after some time I was finally "selected" by the Glam Princess to walk for her in the Detroit Ultimate White Party Fashion Show of 2015!

Curvy Girl Magic

BEAUTIFUL DECORUS FASHION DESIGNER AND MODEL PAULETTE GREEN SPEAKS ON HER MODELING DAYS AND UPCOMING CLOTHING LINE.

by: Cheraee C.

Q. When did you start modeling and what inspired you to pursue modeling?

A. I started modeling in 2008. I love being in front of a camera, been that way since a kid. Growing up I admired everything about fashion. It's so creative and unique and everyone has their own perspective on what's beautiful. I absolutely love it!

Q. So far what is the craziest thing that ever happened to you at a fashion show?

A. There are so many stories I could tell, but I'll stick with just one. The makeup artist and hair stylist for a show didn't show up and the designer wanted our hair a certain way. The hair stylist was supposed to do everybody's hair so all the models was sitting around looking like we just stuck our hand into a socket. We had to think fast so we all grabbed combs, brushes, gel, spritz, edge control, flat irons, and we all did eachother's hair. We made it work and as a modedl that's just what you hav to do.

Q. Do you have a favorite fashion designer mainstream or underground and why are they your favorite?

A. I have so many favorites! I have to say Chamere Payton. I have been one of Chamere's models going on three years now and she will always be my favorite. She is not only my mentor, but my inspiration. Curvy women don't have many choices and opportunities in the fashion world and she makes you feel like the most beautiful woman in the room when you have on one of her pieces. She is hardworking and so dedicated to her brand "Kizzed." She is also very supportive. I am working on building my own clothing line and I can only hope to be as great as her!

Q. How did you meet Chamere and can you tell us aour future clothing line?

A. I met Chamere at a casting call. I walked for her in one of my very first fashion shows. We've been like glue to eachother every since. My clothing line is called "Decorus Designz." Decorous means beautiful in Latin and that's the backbone of my collection. I want women to feel beautiful when

they wear something I made.

Q. When do you plan to launch your brand and where do you plan to sell your line?

A. I showcased my 1st collection last year in August at a fashion show. I'll be showcasing my 2nd collection this coming April. I will have business cards and my website up within the next couple of weeks.

Q. If you could be in any fashion show around the world what would it be and why?

A. It use to be NYFW, but thanks to Chamere for selecting me to model for her at NYFW, she made my dream a reality. I am ever so thankful so my next dream show would be Paris Fashion Week. If you think big and dream big then there is nothing stopping you from chasing every dream you have!

From Glam to Glamourous

THE FASHION DESIGNER AND CEO OF KIZZED CHAMERE PAYTON
SPECIALIZES IN SEXY, CURVY GIRL FASHIONS & COSMETICS

by Cheraee C.

Q. Who was the 1st music artist you designed a piece for, what was the design, and what was the artist's reaction to receiving it?
A.The first music artist I designed for was Lynn Carter. She was performing for the SDM Launch Party downtown. I designed a blush pink sequin gown for her to perform in. Lynn absolutely loved her garment. I created an entire look for her including a clutch, heels, and earrings. Everything coordinated to ensure a complete and glamorous look.

Q. What is the name of your brand and what inspired your brand's name?
A.The name of my brand is Kizzed. The name was inspired by my obsession with kisses and the symbol of lips. My favorite selfie face includes duck lips lol. I wanted to build my brand around what I love. I've always been a plus-sized girl. This is why all of my clothing is dedicated and targeted towards plus-size, curvy women.

Q. Recently, you were a part of New York's Fashion Week. Describe the first and last experiences you've had in New York during this time?
A .My first experience at NYFW was in February of 2015. I took a leap of faith and hoped to take my brand to new heights. My showcase was on Valentine's Day and the experience was surreal. I was able to do what I love on one of the biggest days for love. The response to my brand was phenomenal. I debuted my glitter cosmetics during this season and they were a hit. I've been mass producing my glitter cosmetics every season ever since. My last experience at NYFW was this past February 2017. I have been attending and showcasing at NYFW for the past 5 seasons. NYFW takes place twice a year – every February and September. Over the years, my brand has grown and I've been able to participate in several productions over the course of the famous week – including Plitsz, NYFW The Shows, A Beautiful You Fashion Tour, and WALK Fashion Show. Kizzed showcased in two productions on Saturday, February 11th. The team was also able to schedule and successfully execute several photo shoots with published, agency photographers such as Jaiden Photography. Networking with international fashion professionals from around the globe is eye opening and great exposure for the brand. The experience gets better every season. The squad and I are looking forward to the next season in September 2017.

Q. A lot of people think of the fashion world as just clothes and money. Describe what being a fashion designer all entails.
A.Fashion is much more than clothes and money. Fashion is a sense of self-expression – a form of artistry. Thru fashion, people are able to free express themselves and present a visual character and personality. Being a fashion designer is taking hold of

that expression and using your creativity to express your own version of art. We call this expression a designer's aesthetic. My aesthetic is size, sexy glamour. Glamorous every day wear as well as evening wear is what I'm known for. I promote body confidence. Sexy comes is all shapes, sizes, and colors. My aesthetic pours over into my cosmetic line as well. My cosmetic line features waterproof, smudge-proof glitter lipsticks in over a dozen different shades. Glitter is life.

Q. Describe a time where you designed a piece and the customer was unhappy. How did you handle the customer under the circumstances?

A. I believe every designer has encountered this. I consider myself a very understanding and considerate business woman. Once, I was hired to design a hi-lo skirt for a repeat client. I received deposit and created the skirt based on my most recent measurements for the client. This proved to be a big mistake. The client received the skirt and paid her balance. Once she tried the skirt on, just before her event, she realized that the garment was improperly fitted. I felt terrible. As a designer who provides custom glamour wear, I take pride in delivering a quality product that meets my client's needs. To ease the situation, I completely refunded the client. To rectify the situation, I properly re-created the garment and delivered it to her. Customer satisfaction is extremely important in this field.

Q. A lot of people have or want to have their own fashion brand. Do you feel like your brand is more successful than other fashion brands in your city?

A. The success of a fashion brand is dependent upon the brand's business strategy and business plan. It's tough to directly compare one brand to another – so much factors in. I feel like my brand is just as successful as any other brand could be. For the past three years, my brand has been the core of my lifestyle. I believe the success of my brand reflects the efforts of myself and my team. Kizzed focuses on a niche market, curvy women, and have created a lane of its own. In Detroit, there's a small fashion network and it's all about support. We all are working hard to bring our vision to life and share it with the world. Once we've accomplished that, we've won. Within every fashion designer you will find passion.

Q. Is the fashion world as competitive and overcrowded as the music industry or worse?

A. Yes, even more competitive than the music industry. As they say on Project Runway, one day you're in and the next day you're out. Trends, seasons, target markets and much more make being a top designer a true task. Every designer fighting to be one notch above the rest. Over time, I've realized that resting peacefully in your lane and focusing on your market is what truly makes you a top designer. Competing but not competing at the same time.

Q. Describe the best experience you've had at a fashion show.

A. The best experience I've had at a fashion show was at WALK 13 held here in Detroit at the Eastern Market. It was the first time Kizzed had the opportunity to showcase in the evening show. All other showcases were during the 'Emerging Designer' showcase. I put my all into the collection and it really showed on and off the runway. Behind the scenes, the showcase ran smoothly. Being able to see my brand in lights on the projector screen in front of a sold out crowd gave me life! I was fortunate to have most of my models exclusive to my line – no sharing. The reaction from the crowd and the overflow of admiration after the showcase made for a great end to the evening. It was by far one of my favorite showcases. I have been a part of the WALK Family for years, but this specific show was one of my favorites.

Legends Lose Royalties

DRU HILL IS FIGHTING TO WIN THEIR MUSIC ROYALTIES

by Semaja Turner

The Baltimore R&B group Dru Hill is currently in a lawsuit battle with the music producers of Sony/ATV, 27 Red Music, and EMI after NY district judge Alison Nathan dismissed their second filing. The alleged lawsuit was filed in 2015 on behalf of the group members Woody (James Green), Jazz (Larry Anthony Jr.) and Sisqo (Mark Andrews) claiming a breach of contract. The lawsuit alleges that EMI paid 600,000 dollars to 27 Red Music, which is a company that was hired by the group in 2005 to collect unpaid royalties from 1996-2005. All the members claim they never received any royalties from EMI and EMI wrongfully paid $30,000 dollars of their royalties to 27 Red Music.

The judge found that Dru Hill failed to allege they had an implied contract with both EMI and Sony, and even if they did the NY's Statute of Frauds would not recognize it. This means that contracts of "indefinite duration" like Dru Hill's are deemed to be incapable of being performed within a year, and fall within the Statute of Frauds category.

Despite this second ruling, Dru Hill is not giving up and their royalty issues and court proceedings still remain unresolved.

Underground King of Soul/R&B

AKINYELE THE BLK NIGHT IS REPRESENTING FOR THE TRUE ROOTS OF MOTOWN'S MUSIC CREATIVELY, VISUALLY, LYRICALLY, AND CONSISTENTLY

by Cheraee C.

Q. As a singer what is the biggest stage you would love to perform on and why?

A. The biggest stage is the FOX in Detroit, MI only because it's in my city. A city of broken dreams and promises; they say we don't have it anymore as far as music, but I know we do. For me to make it on one of the biggest stages in my city would be a way to show my people we can make it here without us having to leave our city where it really all started as far as R&B/Soul Music.

Q. What made you want to become independent in every aspect of music? Get your own label, do your own production and etc?

A. In the city I'm from its not a lot of outlets here anymore and very little unity. Motown is not for Detroit when it comes to today's music so it's always been hard for me to find a place that I can call home and do what I want to do musically for myself and others. So me and my brother decided to do our own thing here in Detroit. True Royal Ent is where only royal music gets made. Independent is more work, but also more controlled creativity so I love it. It keeps the raw passion in the music nowadays.

Q. How many music projects have you done independently and what's the most memorable project you've done and why?

A. I've done 9 full mixtapes/projects all on datpiff.com from 2012 to the present. My first project was Can Do It Too, WTF I Feel, Blk To The Future, Song's From A D Boy, Songs For Her, Let The Truth Be Told, Sex Chronicles, R&B Love, and The Gift of Music This Christmas. The most memorable of all I will have to say for me is between Sex Chronicles & The Gift of Music This Christmas. Sex Chronicles because of the vibe of the project in it's entirety, the way people responded to it, and the way it made me feel just putting it together. The Gift of Music This Christmas because it was just beautiful to make music with family and friends and it gives you a different vibe then the same old Christmas music we hear every year around the holidays. It had not been done since Boyz II Men so I did it my way.

Q. When and where are you at your most creative element to make music?

A. I'm creative from every element of life. For me it's not a place it's more of a mood, a vibe, or feelings. What I see, what I hear, what I go through, the love, the hurt, the pain, and passion for something or someone even the hate for something or someone. I know personally for me a lot of my drive comes from hurt, pain, and love that's what I have to share so I pour it all into my music. The best place for me to be musically creative is definitely in my feelings in my lab drinking alone.

Q. Have you ever received an award or recognition for your music and how do you feel about local music awards?

A. As of to date I have not received any awards. I always get recognized for my music whether it's writing, producing, or being an artist myself. The people that know or follow me and my music, my city know what to expect from me that real R&B feel. As far as local music awards I think that's a cool thing to do. It's always a good thing to be recognized by your people in your hometown. That's love long as they keep it 100. We all know the politics and favoritism game.

She Got The Game On Lock

GUCCI RIE TALKS ABOUT HER ROLE IN SOMETHING SHADY, HER NEW SINGLE, AND HER NEWFOUND PASSION IN MODELING & FASHION DESIGNING

by Cheraee C.

Q. Why do you think people treat you like an underdog when you are clearly a female boss with credentials?

A. Well I can't say they treat me like a underdog lol. I think me holding the "diva" title down they know I come with madd confidence, too jealous to appreciate it so they try to downplay me. I allowed it doe, it's totally my fault, but that's goin change that's a promise. Like Game say, "the underdogs on top." They watching! They see me, they know I'm coming! I'm the threat they goin respect #RAPDIVA. Beauty, but a beast at it #swinghair. So if I'm the underdog then watch me put some heat on their butts lol they not ready

Q. You star in a new TV Series called "Something Shady" as Lindsay. What is your favorite attribute Lindsay has?

A. Wow, I love Something Shady and I adore Lindsay. One thing I like about playing the role of Lindsay is that she is a boss chicka with the doe #swinghair. It's a honor to play such a role character and it's a challenge, but somebody gotta do it, why not me?

Q. You just dropped a new single. What is the name of your new single and what motivated your lyrics?

A. My new single is titled "Game On Lock" because that's exactly what I'm going to do. I'm going to slay it all; rap game, fashion game, and film game because I'm a triple threat diva. I'm a rapper, actress, and model so how they goin stop me when I got the key. The people who are trying to hold me back motivated me so if you listen to the song it's fun. You goin dance, but it's a message in it for all the people who want to lock down the game.

Q. Recently you were in a fashion show. Tell us about the show and your experience flexing down the stage?

A. The fashion show was everything and just learning how to strut was a challenge lol, but I did it. When I came out I was shocked on how many people was screaming for me. What a good moment. I met great models, designers, singers, and more. The Fashion Gala was a good thing. Hairdressers and make-up artists came out to slay us. My experience was a lesson saying "Gucci Rie you can be a star baby."

Q. Being a triple threat diva, what trait do you think you will be adding to your skills next?

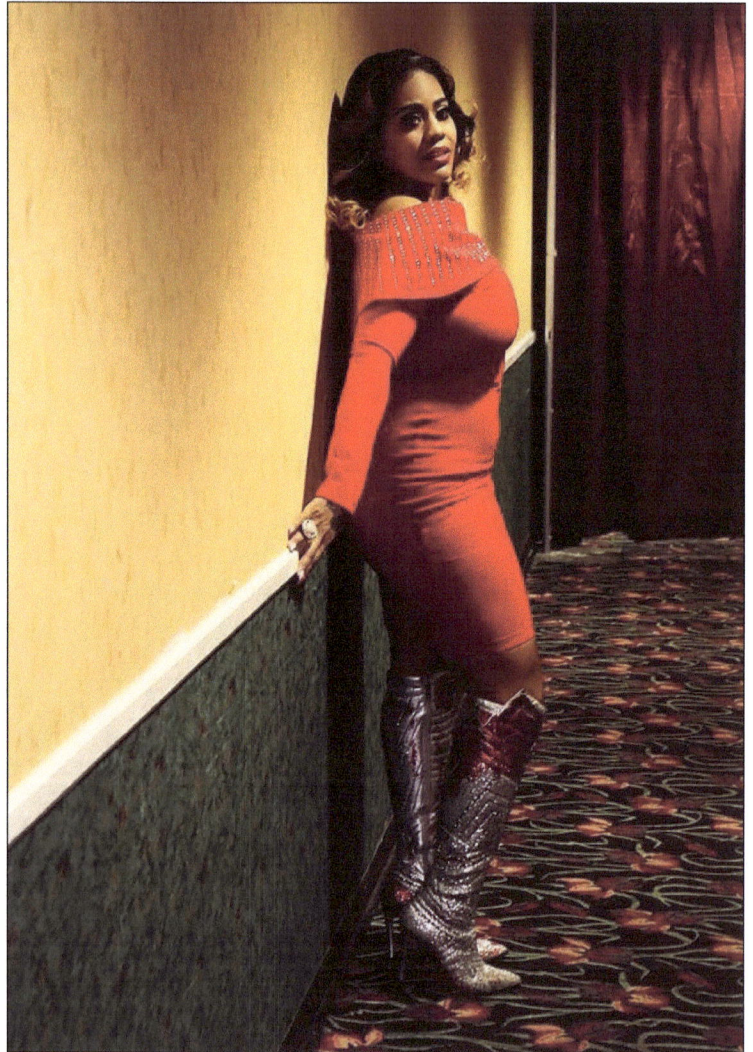

A. I saw this fashion designer make accessories, cool hats, clothes, and boots so I want to tap into my artistic side and begin creating some pieces of my own. Before rap I was into fashion heavy. I always dreamed of owning my own million dollar clothing store. Why you think they call me Gucci? Lol I'm a fashion designer on the rise too, Music and fashion is my medicine in life. So when people make me mad I stay up all night writing or designing clothes. My haters, I mean my confused fans goin make me rich so let me take time to thank them mwahh! I'm a Jill of all trades and they can't handle all of that not fareal. But they better get used to it! Giving all the glory to God! Even doe I talk tuff my heart is good and I remain humble.

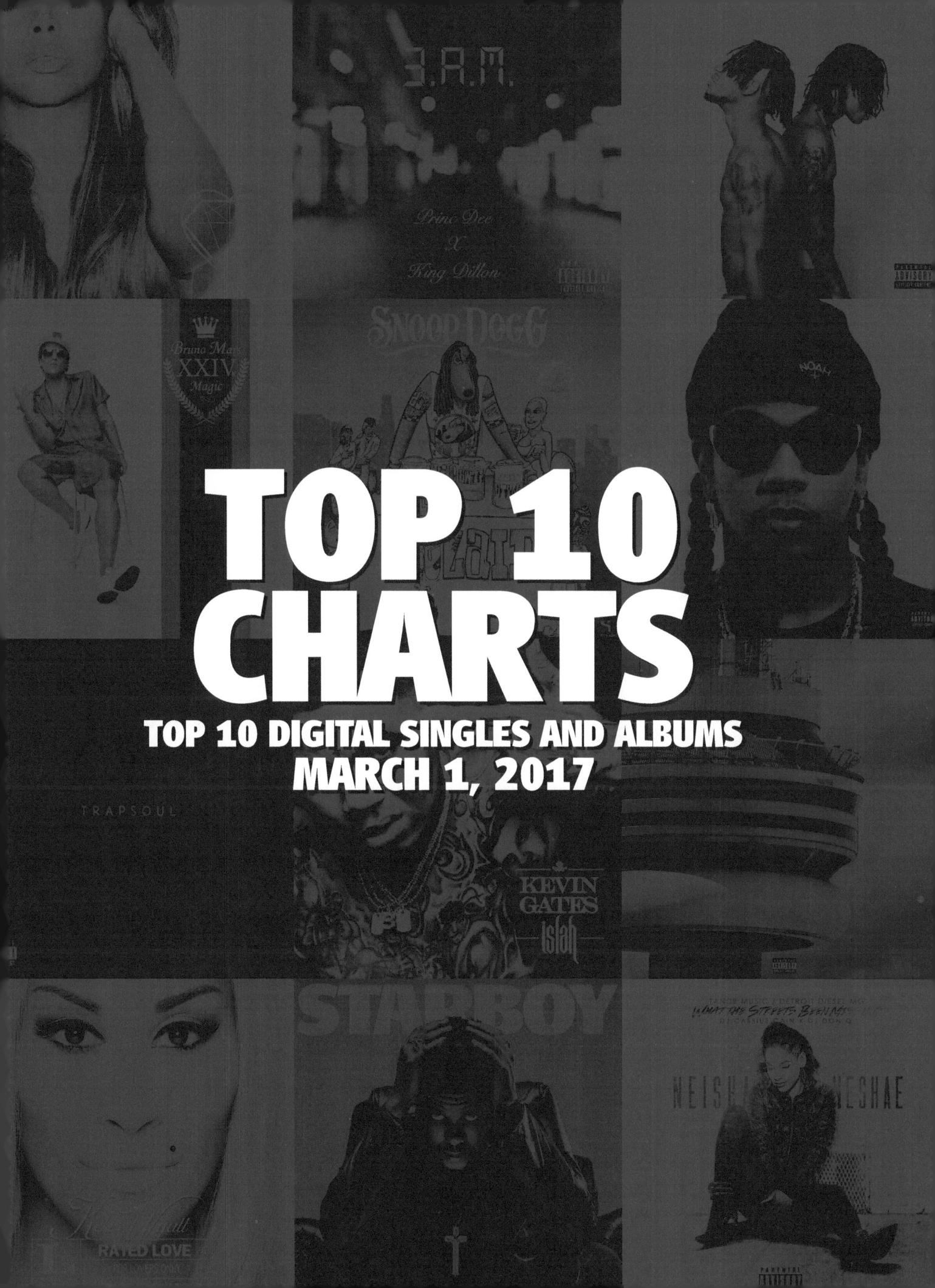

TOP 10 CHARTS

TOP 10 DIGITAL SINGLES AND ALBUMS
MARCH 1, 2017

TOP 10 CHARTS

MIGOS "BAD AND BOUJEE FEATURING LIL UZI VERT" AT THE OFFICIAL VIDEO SHOOT.

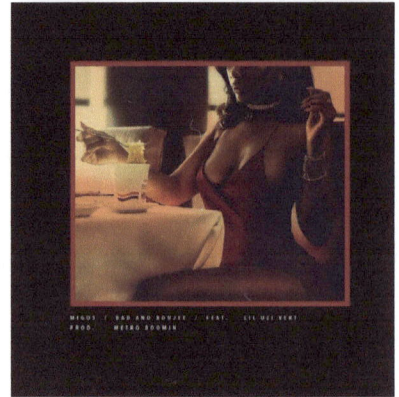

Migos
Bad and Boujee

Coming in at #1 this month, The hottest song on the radio "Bad and Boujee" for all the money gettin ladies.

TOP 10 SINGLES
CHART OF THE MONTH

No.	Artist - Song Title
1	MIGOS - BAD AND BOUJEE
2	BRUNO MARS - 24K MAGIC
3	ZAY HILFIGERRR & ZAYLON MCCALL - JUJU ON THAT BEAT
4	MACHINE GUN KELLY - BAD THINGS
5	DRAKE - FAKE LOVE
6	JP ONE - MILLION
7	YOUNG M.A. - OOOUUU
8	RIHANNA - LOVE ON THE BRAIN
9	BIG SEAN - BOUNCE BACK
10	J. COLE - DEJA VU

TOP 10 ALBUMS
CHART OF THE MONTH

No.	Artist - Album Title
1	BIG SEAN - I DECIDED
2	KEHLANI - SWEETSEXTSAVAGE
3	MIGOS - CULTURE
4	FUTURE - FUTURE
5	THE WEEKND - STARBOY
6	GUCCI MANE - THE RETURN OF EAST ATLANTA SANTA
7	THE WEEKND - STARBOY
8	TI - US OR ELSE (EP)
9	RAE SREMMURD - SREMMLIFE 2
10	LIL UZI VERT - LIL UZI VERT VS. THE WORLD

I Decided
ARTIST: Big Sean
RATING: 5

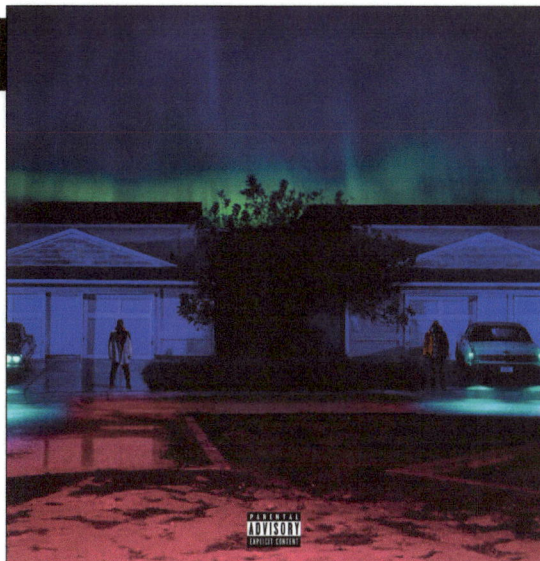

Falling in love with this 14 track Album wasn't difficult to do, when it came to the 28 year old music artist raised out of Detroit, MI. Where he reflects on life, the media, and obtaining privacy and peace with his fourth studio Album "I Decided". We get enticing variety of beats from producers DJ Mustard, Key Wane, Metro Boomin and many others. With features from Jeremiah, The Dream, Flint Chozen Choir, Twenty88, Migos, Starrah, and the Rap God Eminem, and Big Sean delivers witty, clever wordplay, catchy hooks, and that classic "Finally Famous" delivery. Discussing the impact his family has had on his career, failed relationships, making sacrifices to get to the top of the hip hop industry, and the media's invasion of privacy, not knowing how to keep the questions focused about the music. Tracks such as "No Favors" ft. Eminem and "Bounce Back" and "Moves" give off a strong hip hop feel with bar after bar that will force you to rewind the track just to catch what went over your head. Favorite track: "Halfway Off the Balcony" Illustrates balancing his mental state, music career, women and being a public figure with how stressful holding the weight of others fates can be with his lyrics; metaphorically rethinking life. "I Decided" depicts that happiness and blessings are worth more than money and when it comes down to finalizing decisions, you become a better man. Really great album!! Go Purchase & check out Big Sean's 4th Studio Album "I Decided" on iTunes!

"I Can't Spend My Whole Life Looking At The Same Ceiling Fan
When I Feel Like I Ain't Got No Ceilings Man! If I Ain't Special Why I Feel It Then?"

SweetSexySavage
ARTIST: Kehlani
RATING: 4

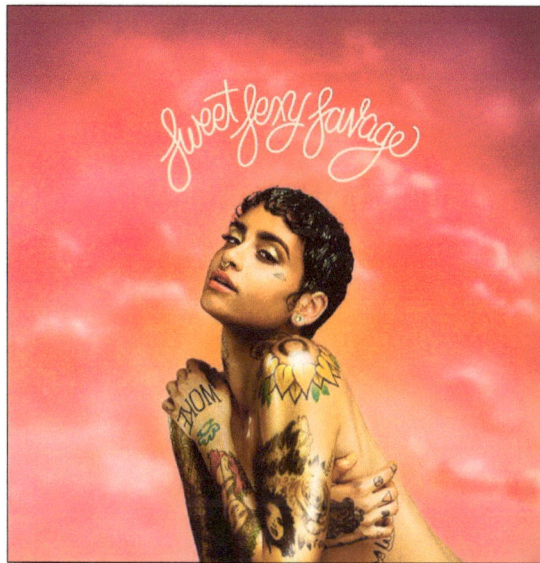

The 21 year old music artist from Oakland, California brings us listeners a 2017 version of 90's RnB with her Debut album "SweetSexySavage"! Kehlani's "SweetSexySavage" title reference to TLC's 1994 sophomore album "CrazySexyCool". The Production was very dope & alluring, Special shout out to Pop & Oak and producer Jahaan Sweet, for a great project with others. Sampling from Akon, New Edition, Rhian Sheehan, and the great & dearly missed Aaliyah, Kehlani was able to gather an abundance of lyrical content which contains amazing skits of empowering, wise words from different women to introduce the next track. Kehlani's harmonious mix of RnB and Pop allows listeners to see her perspective with the approach of being an young adult and coping with the music industry, going through trail and error with relationships, while learning what love truly means, all while coming into her own. Tracks like "Keep On", "Advice", and "Hold Me By The Heart" gave me the "Sweet" vibe while Tracks like "Distraction", "Undercover", and the hit single "CRZY" gave off that "Sexy" feel, and "Personal", "In My Feelings", and "Do U Dirty" reflects the "Savage" side. It's great to give the new generation a type of 90's style RnB that can be appreciated, and it's nostalgic for myself to listen through this 19 track album. Great album Miss Parrish. Check out Kehlani's Debut Album "SweetSexySavage" on iTunes and Spotify!

"My condolences to anyone who has ever lost me, and to anyone who got lost in me or to anyone who ever felt they took a loss with me, my apologies for the misunderstanding." - Reyna Biddy

Phoenix Nicole
is a beautiful video
model from Detroit, MI.

instagram
@phoenix_nicole21

The Real Focus

A Police officer in the movie True Religion from Detroit MI.

instagram

@therealbfocus

HEELS & SKILLZ

Photography by
@barearmy

HEELS & SKILLZ

Gangsta Doll

A video model in the movie True Religion from Detroit MI.

instagram
gangstadolll

Photography by
@barearmy

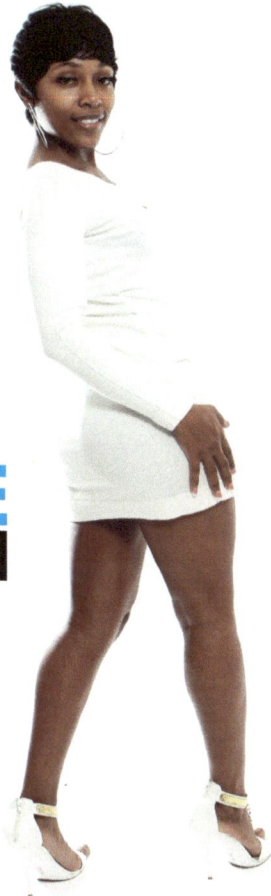

Cheraee's Corner
WHAT HAPPENED TO WOMEN LOVING THEIR NATURAL SELVES?

by Cheraee C.

Women across the globe are too content with using plastic surgery as their flaw reducer and confident booster. There are a handful of women who strive in upholding naturalness despite what standard society paints for a woman's body. Having a bigger butt, bigger boobs, smaller waistlines, or even simple augmentation procedures is becoming a norm. Women are spending tax money to do it, women are stripping to do it, and women are flying from overseas to the U.S. just to do it.

Too many lives are being lost to these unnecessary body enhancements and women are becoming too frivolous with money and technology. Why can't we as woman be comfortable in our skin with our natural bodies? Just because aesthetics surgeons and clinics exist doesn't mean we have to utilize them. There shouldn't be any Dr. Miami's or booty guru's. People shouldn't be allowed to change eye colors or have plastic surgery unless it's for medical or government reasons.

What happened to women believing sayings like, "beauty is skin deep" or "beauty is in the eye of the beholder?" If you don't like something about yourself work it out with God and a gym.

NEXT 2 BLOW

RAIL FRESH

Q. Your single "Feel It" is a remake/cover of the Dale hit "Soulful Moaning." What made you cover that song?

A. Its more of a remake than a cover. When I first heard the beat I noticed the sample and thought it was perfect with Dale being a Detroit native as well and just wanted to add a little of my personality to a classic. It was definitely in my mind a good look for putting on for my city and what we have to offer.

Q. You seem to be a master of branding. Why do you think it's important artists stay connected with DJ's and who is your DJ?

A. I haven't even mastered it yet, but I'm working on it lol, but DJ's are the lifeline and a lot know that, but a lot abuse it. DJ's and artists just naturally go hand in hand and it's a must. My DJ I'm working with is DJ Diz Dre, but as far as an official DJ I don't have one. I'm a true independent, free flowing artist so I connect with as many genuine DJ's as I can.

Q. Artists are usually multi-talented. What other gifts do you have besides music?

A. As far as music I developed an awareness for rapping thru writing because anything anyone has ever heard from Rail Fresh was written by me but, I produce, but that's not my lane. I just do enough to get my vision across. I play guitar a little and I'm still learning. I hope to be able to say in the future I can do almost errthang musically.

Q. If you decide to remake another R&B legend, what song would you do next and why?

A. Maybe Frankie Beverly, but a lot of people been using them lately so Imma go with Musiq Soulchild or Joe. That's what I grew up on and was most comfortable with singing even though I developed a newer type of style I keep their same feel in my music because it flows right for me, but they had it first lol.

Q. Is it any female artist in the underground scene you would like to collab with and why?

A. Female artists that I've heard are ok, but I can't call off hand which one I'd work with. I need to do a lil more research, but Most Wanted I believe is her name and she's tight. The power and tone of her voice is nice. I became a fan of hers ever since I've heard her on a track. I'll definitely work with her.

Q. What was the first single you released as an artist, what did you like/dislike about the single, and what outlet did you release it on?

A. My very first single was called Money on my Mind. I ended up getting Icewear Vezzo on the remix and that made me really love it. I didn't really have any dislikes except looking back now I think my sound has developed. I was only 20 at the time and it released on soodetroitmag.

Q. What have you learned so far being an independent artist in the music industry?
A. That's it's not about how good you are anymore. I'm learning the marketing and business aspect of the industry. I also learned not to trust everybody. Paperwork is a must to protect yourself because at the end of the day everybody is for themselves.

Q. Do you have a mentor/mentors in the industry to assist you along the way?
A. Nope, it's just me and my engineer.

Q. How has your style evolved over the years and through the music you have done.
A. When I first started you couldn't tell me I wasn't part of the Doughboys Cashout lol. I feel I have developed an industry and universal sound now.

Q. What female artist in the industry now would you like to work with and why?
A. Dreezy. I was a fan of her from her first record break a band before her mixtape. She's the dopest out right now to me and I feel like we represent the same thing.

NEXT 2 BLOW

BRIAA DURPEE

SNAP SHOTS

Email Your Snap Shots to
snapshots@sdmlive.com

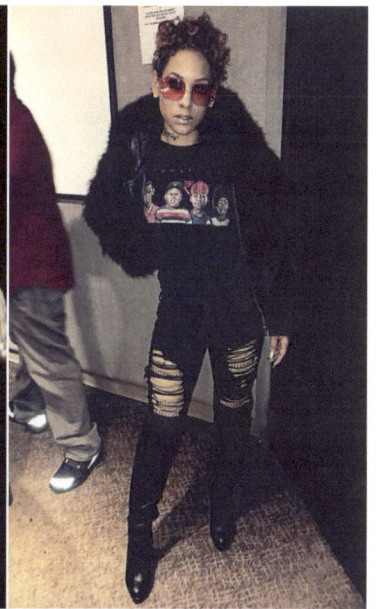

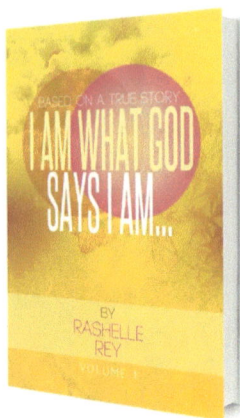

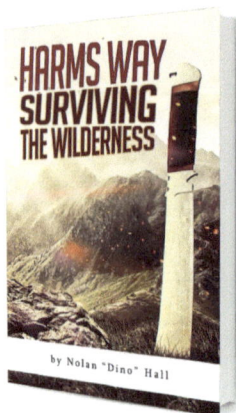

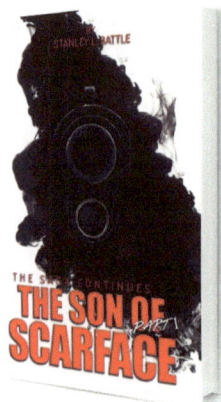

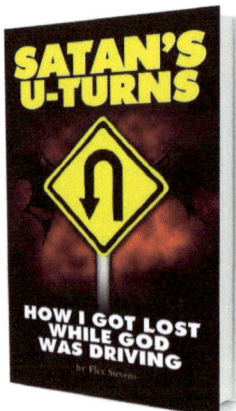

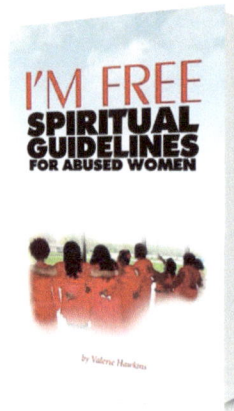

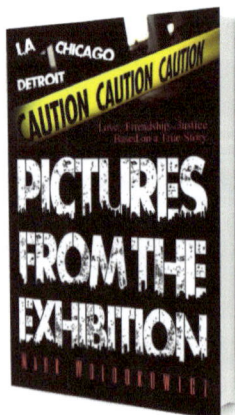

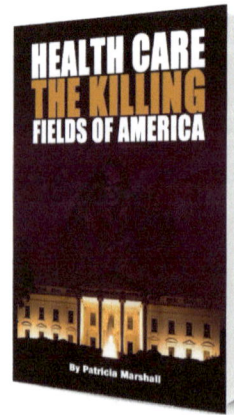

THE ALL NEW STYLE OF MAGAZINE-BOOKS

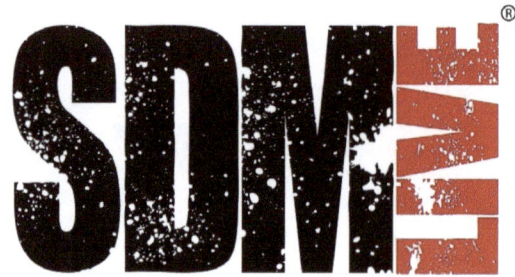

SDMLIVE ®

www.ingramcontent.com/pod-product-compliance
Lightning Source LLC
Chambersburg PA
CBHW041526070426
42452CB00036B/32